CATS ARE BETTER THAN MEN

CATS ARE BETTER THAN MEN

BEVERLY GUHL

Hodder & Stoughton

LONDON SYDNEY AUCKLAND

First published in the United States of America in 1994
by Doubleday, a division of Bantam Doubleday Dell Publishing Group, Inc.

First published in Great Britain in 1994
by Hodder and Stoughton, a division of Hodder Headline PLC

10 9 8 7 6 5 4 3 2 1

British Library Cataloguing in Publication Data
Guhl, Beverly
    Cats are Better Than Men
    I. Title
    815. 5402
ISBN 0—340—67175—0

Printed and bound in Great Britain by
Mackays of Chatham PLC, Chatham, Kent

Hodder and Stoughton Ltd
A division of Hodder Headline PLC
338 Euston Road
London NW1 3BH

TO CATS AND MEN EVERYWHERE,
WITHOUT WHOM THIS BOOK COULD NOT HAVE BEEN WRITTEN

Beverly Guhl has designed and marketed everything from greeting cards and stationery to decorative magnets, record albums, and mugs. She has also written and illustrated two previous books: *Purrfect Parenting* and *Teenage Years—A Parent's Survival Guide*. The mother of two college-age children and one cat, she lives in Austin, Texas, where she is Director of Graphics for the Texas Department of Protective and Regulatory Services. Although a staunch supporter of human rights and gender equality, she says she would probably vote for a cat if one ran for office.

CATS ARE BETTER THAN MEN

They never complain about your weight.

They never accuse you of being
too emotional.

They can show their emotions.

They take an interest in your work.

They never leave the seat up.

They don't care how much money you spend.

They don't use up all the hot water.

They don't need to see a shrink.

They always let you know when
they plan to go out.

They're eager to please you.

They never have other plans.

They heartily approve of your
taste in furnishings.

They don't complain about work
or their boss.

They don't talk about themselves.

They're kissable, and there's
no beard burn.

They think you look just fine
without makeup.

They don't require closet space.

They don't cheat on you.

They listen to your problems.

They never try to make you
feel guilty.

They don't care what you wear to bed.

They don't eat up all the food
in the fridge.

They never say they'll call
then never call.

They LO_VE_ yard work.

They like to snuggle all night long.

They never break dates at
the last minute.

They're never late for dinner.

Their grooming habits are
never in question.

They never complain about your cooking.

...or your friends...

...or your new hairdo.

They don't work weekends.

They never ask to borrow money.

They <u>LOVE</u> leftovers.

They think you look wonderful
in the morning.

They can take care of themselves
when you go out.

They don't leave smelly socks
all over the house.

They never make you feel stupid.

They're always bringing you gifts.

They don't hide behind a newspaper.

They love your fuzzy terry bathrobe as much as you do.

They don't care if you don't shave
your legs for days or weeks.

They LO<u>VE</u> your mother.

They have impeccable table manners.

They're never on the phone.

They like romance novels, too.

They never complain about your housekeeping.

They don't watch sports on TV.

CLICK

They love dinner parties.

They don't hog the covers or snore.